Gastric Sleeve Bariatric

Cookbook UK 2023

Simple and Delicious Recipes for a Fresh Approach to Weight Loss and Healthier
Living & Keep the Weight Off

Chloe Saunders

CONTENTS

INTRODUCTION

Gastric Sleeve Diet

If you are planning to have gastric sleeve surgery you will need to follow a specific and strict diet that starts two weeks before the procedure.

Your gastric sleeve pre-op diet aims to reduce your liver size and weight to make the operation easier.

Your gastric sleeve post-op diet will help you to recover from surgery and avoid complications.

You will move through the post-op diet stages of liquids, pureed and soft foods, to a final diet of healthy protein rich, low calorie solid foods that you will need to continue for life to achieve and maintain your weight loss goals.

The success of your gastric sleeve surgery will depend on your ability to stick to a healthy diet and lifestyle.

Your bariatric team will give you information on your gastric sleeve diet and offer support throughout your weight loss journey.

Pre-gastric Sleeve Diet

If you are overweight, your liver will be too. Your liver is found right next to your stomach, so a larger liver makes gastric sleeve surgery more difficult and increases your risk of complications.

Your liver can shrink in size very quickly. If you follow a strict pre-op diet two weeks before your scheduled gastric sleeve surgery date, your liver will shrink and your procedure will be safer, quicker and easier. This diet also prepares you for your gastric sleeve post-op diet.

A gastric sleeve pre-op diet typically reduces your calorie intake, lowers your carbohydrate consumption, and eliminates sugar from your diet. Two days before your surgery, you can expect to move to a clear liquid diet avoiding caffeine and carbonated drinks.

It is important that you follow your weight loss surgeon's recommended two-week gastric sleeve pre-op diet. Your surgeon may also recommend that you take daily bariatric multivitamins to ensure your body gets all the nutrients it requires.

Post Operation Diet

After your gastric sleeve operation your body will need nutrients to heal your wounds and help you recover fully.

You will pass through five phases of eating that include: clear liquid, full liquid, pureed, soft food, and finally an ongoing protein-rich nourishing diet. You can expect to spend around one week in each phase. You should not skip phases.

Long term diet tips following gastric sleeve surgery

You will need to continue eating a healthy, high protein, low fat, calorie-controlled diet for the rest of your life to achieve and maintain your weight goals.

Some top tips include:

- Keep to three small meals a day.
- Have protein in each meal and eat it first.
- Introduce new foods one by one.
- Take a tablet form daily vitamin and mineral supplement as directed by your bariatric team. You will also require vitamin B12 injections (1mg) once every three months.
- Eat slowly and chew your food thoroughly. The more you chew, the easier your food is to swallow and digest.
- Plan your meals so you are not tempted by off-diet foods.
- Drink plenty of water and always have some water to hand.
- If you feel hungry between meals try taking a drink first as your body may be mistaking hunger with thirst. If you are still hungry then have a small snack such as a piece of fruit or a low-fat yoghurt.
- Ask for half portions at restaurants – it may be discounted and it will prevent you from being tempted to overeat.

Foods to avoid:

- Food with empty calories – make wise diet choices and avoid foods with little or no nutritional value.
- Alcohol - is high in calories and your alcohol absorption will dramatically increase after surgery.

- Fizzy drinks - as they cause bloating and can increase your small stomach size.
- High fat foods – they may make you feel nauseous and will not help you to lose weight.
- Tough meats - are hard to chew and hard to digest.

Things to avoid:

- Avoid eating and drinking together - wait at least thirty minutes between eating and drinking. Drinking fluids with meals may lead to an overfull stomach and vomiting. It can also stretch your stomach and "wash" your food through too quickly so that you don't sense the early signs of fullness and may lead to over eating.
- Avoid overeating - stop eating when you feel satisfied. Overeating will stretch your stomach pouch and may make you vomit.
- Avoid grazing - this often adds extra calories to your controlled diet. It also interferes with your body's ability to burn fat as insulin levels will be consistently raised

Breakfast Recipes

Quinoa Bowls

Servings: 2   **Cooking Time: 25 minutes**

Ingredients:

- 1 sliced peach
- 1/3 cup quinoa
- 1 cup low fat milk
- ½ tsp. vanilla extract
- 2 tsps. natural stevia
- 12 raspberries
- 14 blueberries
- 2 tsps. honey

Directions:

1. Add natural stevia, 2/3 cup milk and quinoa to a saucepan, and stir to combine.
2. Over medium high heat, bring to a boil then cover and reduce heat to a low simmer for a further 20 minutes.
3. Grease and preheat grill to medium. Grill peach slices for about a minute per side. Set aside.
4. Heat remaining milk in the microwave and set aside.
5. Split cooked quinoa evenly between 2 serving bowls and top evenly with remaining Ingredients:. Enjoy!

Nutrition: Per Serves: Calories: 180, Fat: 4g, Carbs: 36g, Protein: 4.5g

Scrambled Eggs

Ingredients:

- 3 eggs, lightly beaten
- 2 tbsp chives, chopped
- ½ cup ricotta
- 1 tbsp butter
- Pepper
- Salt

Directions:

1. Melt butter in a pan over medium heat.
2. In a bowl, whisk together eggs, chives, ricotta, pepper, and salt and pour into the pan.
3. Gently stir egg mixture until eggs are cooked and scrambled, about 5 minutes.
4. Serve and enjoy.

Nutrition: Per Serves: Calories 464 Fat 34.5 g Carbohydrates 7.7 g Sugar 1.5 g Protein 31.1 g Cholesterol 560 mg

Mushroom Frittata

 Servings: 2　　 **Cooking Time: 30 minutes**

Ingredients:

- 6 eggs, lightly beaten
- 2 oz butter
- 2 oz green onion, chopped
- 3 oz fresh spinach
- 5 oz mushrooms, sliced
- 4 oz feta cheese, crumbled
- Pepper
- Salt

Directions:

1. Preheat the oven to 350 F/ 180 C.
2. Whisk eggs, cheese, pepper, and salt in a bowl.
3. Melt butter in a pan over medium heat.
4. Add mushrooms and green onion to the pan and sauté for 5-10 minutes.
5. Add spinach and sauté for 2 minutes.
6. Pour egg mixture to the pan.
7. Bake in preheated oven for 20 minutes.
8. Serve and enjoy.

Nutrition: Per Serves: Calories 680 Fat 56.7 g Carbohydrates 8.3 g Sugar 4.3 g Protein 38 g Cholesterol 612 mg

High-Protein Pancakes

 Servings: 4　　🍲 **Cooking Time: 5 minutes**

Ingredients:

- 3 eggs
- 1 cup low-fat cottage cheese
- ⅓ cup whole-wheat pastry flour
- 1½ tablespoons coconut oil, melted
- Nonstick cooking spray
- Post-Op
- ½ pancake
- 1 to 2 pancakes

Directions:

1. In large bowl, lightly whisk the eggs.
2. Whisk in the cottage cheese, flour, and coconut oil just until combined.
3. Heat a large skillet or griddle over medium heat, and lightly coat with the cooking spray.
4. Using a measuring cup, pour ⅓ cup of batter into the skillet for each pancake. Cook for 2 to 3 minutes, or until bubbles appear across the surface of each pancake. Flip over the pancakes and cook for 1 to 2 minutes on the other side, or until golden brown.
5. Serve immediately.

Nutrition: Per Serves: Calories: 182; Total fat: 10g; Protein: 12g; Carbs: 10g; Fiber: 3g; Sugar: 1g; Sodium: 68mg

Guava Smoothie

 Servings: 2   **Cooking Time: 5-7 minutes**

Ingredients:

- 1 cup guava, seeds removed, chopped
- 1 cup baby spinach, finely chopped
- 1 banana, peeled and sliced
- 1 tsp fresh ginger, grated½ medium-sized mango, peeled and chopped
- 2 cups water

Directions:

1. Peel the guava and cut in half. Scoop out the seeds and wash it. Cut into small pieces and set aside.
2. Rinse the baby spinach thoroughly under cold running water. Drain well and torn into small pieces. Set aside. Peel the banana and chop into small chunks. Set aside.
3. Peel the mango and cut into small pieces. Set aside.
4. Now, combine guava, baby spinach, banana, ginger, and mango in a juicer and process until well combined. Gradually add water and blend until all combined and creamy.
5. Transfer to a serving glass and refrigerate for 20 minutes before serving.Enjoy!

Nutrition: Per Serves: Net carbs 39.1 g;Fiber 7.8 g;Fats 1.4 g;Fatsr 2 g;Calories 166

Cherry Avocado Smoothie

 Servings: 3 🍲 **Cooking Time: 5 minutes**

Ingredients:

- ½ ripe avocado, chopped
- 1 cup fresh cherries
- 1 cup coconut water, sugar-free
- 1 whole lime

Directions:

1. Peel the avocado and cut in half. Remove the pit and chop into bite-sized pieces. Reserve the rest in the refrigerator. Set aside.

2. Rinse the cherries under cold running water using a large colander. Cut each in half and remove the pits. Set aside.

3. Peel the lime and cut in half. Set aside.

4. Now, combine avocado, cherries, coconut water, and lime in a blender. Pulse to combine and transfer to a serving glass.

5. Add few ice cubes and refrigerate for 10 minutes before serving.

Nutrition: Per Serves: Net carbs 17 g;Fiber 3.8 g;Fats 6.8 g;Fatsr 3 g;Calories 128

Easy Baked Salmon

🥣 **Servings: 4**   🍲 **Cooking Time: 16 minutes**

Ingredients:

- 4 salmon fillets
- 1 lemon zest
- 1 tsp sea salt
- 3 oz olive oil
- 1 garlic clove, minced
- 1 tsp fresh dill, chopped
- 1 tbsp fresh parsley, chopped
- 1/8 tsp white pepper

Directions:

1. Preheat the oven at 200°C.
2. Place all Ingredients: except salmon fillet in microwave safe bowl and microwave for 45 seconds.
3. Stir well until combine.
4. Place salmon fillets on parchment lined baking dish.
5. Spread evenly olive oil and herb mixture over each salmon fillet.
6. Place in preheated oven and bake for 15 minutes.
7. Serve and enjoy.

Nutrition: Per Serves: Calories: 408, Fat: 30.9 g, Carbohydrates: 0.5 g, Sugar: 0 g, Protein: 34.7 g, Cholesterol: 78 mg

Carrot cake oatmeal

Ingredients:

- ½ - cup unsweetened almond milk
- 1 - small carrot, peeled and finely grated
- 1/3 - cup rolled oats
- 1 -tablespoon raisins
- 1 - teaspoon honey
- ¼ - teaspoon vanilla extract
- 1 - pinch cinnamon
- 1 - pinch salt
- 1 ½ - tablespoons peanut butter
- 1/3 - cup low-fat cottage cheese

Directions:

1. In a bit pot, be part of almond milk, half cup water, carrot, oats, raisins, nectar, vanilla, cinnamon, and salt. Heat to the factor of boiling, at that point, reduce to stew and cook, mixing sporadically, until thick and oats are stout, 5 to 7minutes.
2. Blend inside the nutty unfold and take out from the heat.
3. Top cereal with curds and extra cinnamon.

Nutrition: Per Serves: Calories 423; fat 17g; carbs 51g; protein 21g

Sweet Millet Congee

Servings: 4 **Cooking Time: 1 hours 15 minutes**

Ingredients:

- 1 c. Millet
- 5 c. Water
- 1 c. Diced sweet potato
- 1 tsp. Cinnamon
- 2 tbsps. Stevia
- 1 diced apple
- ¼ c. Honey

Directions:

1. In a deep pot, add stevia, sweet potato, cinnamon, water and millet, then stir to combine.
2. Bring to boil over high heat, then reduce to a simmer on low for an hour or until water is fully absorbed and millet is cooked.
3. Stir in remaining ingredients and serve.

Nutrition: Per Serves: Calories: 136, Fat: 1g, Carbs: 28.5g, Protein: 3.1g

Breakfast Kale Muffins

 Servings: 8   **Cooking Time: 30 minutes**

Ingredients:

- 6 eggs, lightly beaten
- 1/2 cup unsweetened coconut milk
- 1/4 cup chives, chopped
- 1 cup kale, chopped
- Pepper
- Salt

Directions:

1. Preheat the oven to 350 F/ 180 C.
2. Spray a muffin tray with cooking spray and set aside.
3. Add all ingredients into the mixing bowl and whisk to combine.
4. Pour mixture into the prepared muffin tray and bake for 30 minutes.
5. Serve and enjoy.

Nutrition: Per Serves: Calories 95 Fat 7 g Carbohydrates 2 g Sugar 1 g Protein 5 g Cholesterol 140 mg

Veggie Egg Scramble

Servings: 1   **Cooking Time: 10 minutes**

Ingredients:

- 3 eggs, lightly beaten
- 1/4 cup bell peppers, chopped
- 4 mushrooms, chopped
- 1 tbsp olive oil
- 1/2 cup spinach, chopped
- Pepper
- Salt

Directions:

1. Heat 1/2 tablespoon of oil in a pan over medium heat.
2. Add vegetables and sauté for 5 minutes.
3. Heat remaining oil in another pan over medium heat.
4. Add eggs and stir until egg is scrambled and cooked, about 5 minutes. Season with pepper and salt.
5. Add sautéed vegetables in egg and stir well.
6. Serve and enjoy.

Nutrition: Per Serves: Calories 334 Fat 26 g Carbohydrates 6 g Sugar 3 g Protein 19 g Cholesterol 490 mg

Very Berry Muesli

Ingredients:

- 1 c. Oats
- 1 c. Fruit flavored yogurt
- ½ c. Milk
- 1/8 tsp. Salt
- ½ c. Dried raisins
- ½ c. Chopped apple
- ½ c. Frozen blueberries
- ¼ c. Chopped walnuts

Directions:

1. Combine yogurt, salt and oats together in a medium bowl, mix well, then cover the mixture tightly.
2. Place in the refrigerator to cool for 6 hours.
3. Add raisins, and apples the gently fold.
4. Top with walnuts and serve. Enjoy!

Nutrition: Per Serves: Calories: 198, Carbs: 31.2g, Fat: 4.3g, Protein: 6g

Apple pie oatmeal

Servings: 1   **Cooking Time: 25 minutes**

Ingredients:

- 1 - cup 2 percent milk
- ½ - medium apple, cored and chopped
- 1/3 - cup rolled oats
- 1 - teaspoon maple syrup
- ¼ - teaspoon vanilla extract
- 1 - pinch cinnamon
- 1 - pinch salt
- 20 - almonds, chopped

Directions:

1. In a bit pot, be part of milk and cleaved apple. Heat to the point of boiling, at that point lessen to a stew and prepare dinner, mixing sometimes, till apple starts off evolved to relax, round 5 minutes.
2. Include oats, syrup, vanilla, cinnamon, and salt. Heat to the factor of boiling, at that factor, lessen to a stew and cook until oats are full, 5 to 7minutes extra.
3. Top with slashed almonds.

Nutrition: Per Serves: Calories: 413Fat: 18g;Carbs: 49g;Sugar: 25g;Protein: 17g

Almond Oatmeal

 Servings: 1   **Cooking Time: 10 minutes**

Ingredients:

- 1/2 cup rolled oats
- 1 tbsp almond butter
- 1/2 cup unsweetened almond milk
- 1 tbsp cranberry sauce
- 1/4 tsp cinnamon
- 1/2 cup water

Directions:

1. Add oats, water, and almond milk in a small saucepan and cook over medium-high heat until thickened.
2. Remove from heat and add almond butter and cinnamon and stir well.
3. Top with cranberry sauce and serve.

Nutrition: Per Serves: Calories 278 Fat 13.4 g Carbohydrates 32.8 g Sugar 1.4 g Protein 9.3 g Cholesterol 0 mg

Veggie Quiche Muffins

 Servings: 12 🍲 **Cooking Time: 50 minutes**

Ingredients:

- ¾ c. Shredded cheddar
- 1c. Green onion
- 1 c. Chopped broccoli
- 1 c. Diced tomatoes
- 2 c. Milk
- 4 eggs
- 1 c. Pancake mix
- 1 tsp. Oregano
- ½ tsp. Salt
- ½ tsp. Pepper

Directions:

1. Set oven to 375 degrees f, and lightly grease a cup muffin tin with oil.
2. Sprinkle tomatoes, broccoli, onions and cheddar into muffin cups.
3. Combine remaining ingredients in a medium bowl, whisk to combine then pour evenly on top of veggies.
4. Set to bake in preheated oven for about 40 minutes or until golden brown.
5. Allow to cool slightly (about 5 minutes) then serve. Enjoy!

Nutrition: Per Serves: Calories: 58.8, Fat: 3.2g, Carbs: 2.9g, Protein: 5.1g

Lunch and Dinner Recipes

Dijon Potato Salad

Servings: 5   **Cooking Time: 20 minutes**

Ingredients:

- 1 lb. potatoes
- 1/2 lime juice
- 2 tbsp olive oil
- 2 tbsp fresh dill, chopped
- 2 tbsp chives, minced
- 1/2 tbsp vinegar
- 1 tbsp Dijon mustard
- 1/2 lime zest
- Pepper
- Salt

Directions:

1. Add water in a large pot and bring to boil.
2. Add potatoes in boiling water and cook for 15 minutes or until tender. Drain well and set aside.
3. In a small bowl, whisk together vinegar, mustard, lime zest, lime juice, olive oil, dill, and chives.
4. Peel potatoes and diced and transfer in mixing bowl.
5. Pour vinegar mixture over potatoes and stir to coat.
6. Season with pepper and salt.
7. Serve and enjoy.

Nutrition: Per Serves: Calories 115;Fat 6 g;Carbohydrates 15 g;Sugar 1 g;Protein 2 g;Cholesterol 0 mg

Rosemary garlic pork roast

 Servings: 6   **Cooking Time: 1 hours 10 minutes**

Ingredients:

- 4 lbs. Pork loin roast, boneless
- 4 garlic cloves, peeled
- 2 lemon juice
- 1/4 cup fresh sage leaves
- 1/3 cup fresh rosemary leaves
- 1 tbsp salt

Directions:

1. Add sage, rosemary, garlic, lemon juice, and salt into the blender and blend until smooth.
2. Rub herb paste all over roast and place on hot grill.
3. Grill for 1 hour.
4. Sliced and serve.

Nutrition: Per Serves: Calories 655;Fat 30 g;Carbohydrates 5 g;Sugar 1 g;Protein 88 g;Cholesterol 246 mg

Red Orange Salad

Ingredients:

- Fresh lettuce leaves, rinsed
- 1 small cucumber sliced
- ½ red bell pepper, sliced
- 1 cup frozen seafood mix
- 1 onion, peeled and finely chopped
- 3 garlic cloves, crushed
- ¼ cup fresh orange juice
- 5 tbsp extra virgin olive oil
- Salt to taste

Directions:

1. Heat up 3 tbsp of extra virgin olive oil over medium-high temperature. Add chopped onion and crushed garlic. Stir fry for about 5 minutes.
2. Reduce the heat to minimum and add 1 cup of frozen seafood mix. Cover and cook for about 15 minutes, until soft. Remove from the heat and allow it to cool for a while.
3. Meanwhile, combine the vegetables in a bowl. Add the remaining 2 tbsp of olive oil, fresh orange juice and a little salt. Toss well to combine.
4. Top with seafood mix and serve immediately.

Nutrition: Per Serves: Calories: 206, Protein: 7g, Total Carbs: 13.1g , Dietary Fibers: 1.8g, Total Fat: 14.6g

Skinny Chicken Pesto Bake

 Servings: 4   **Cooking Time: 35 minutes**

Ingredients:

- 160 oz. Skinless chicken
- 1 tsps. Basil
- 1 sliced tomato
- 6 tbsps. Shredded mozzarella cheese
- 2 tsps. Grated parmesan cheese

Directions:

1. Cut chicken into thin strips.
2. Set oven to 400 degrees f. Prepare a baking sheet by lining with parchment paper.
3. Lay chicken strips on prepared baking sheet. Top with pesto and brush evenly over chicken pieces.
4. Set to bake until chicken is fully cooked (about 15 minutes).
5. Garnish with parmesan cheese, mozzarella, and tomatoes.
6. Set to continue baking until cheese melts (about 5 minutes).

Nutrition: Per Serves: Calories: 180, Fat: 4g, Carbs: 36g, Protein: 4.5g

Nutty Crunch Porridge

Servings: 1   **Cooking Time: 10 minutes**

Ingredients:

- 1 cup almond milk
- 3 tablespoons farina breakfast porridge mix (such as Cream of Wheat or Malt-O-Meal)
- Dash of salt
- 1 tablespoons sliced almonds (toasted)

Directions:

1. In a small saucepan, heat almond milk to a simmer (do not boil).
2. Whisk farina into milk until smooth.
3. Reduce heat and simmer, uncovered, until porridge is thickened, about 2 minutes, stirring occasionally.
4. Stir salt into porridge. Pour porridge into a bowl and sprinkle with almonds to serve. Enjoy!

Nutrition: Per Serves: Calories: 155; Total Fat: 11g; Saturated Fat: 1g; Protein: 5g; Carbs: 10g; Fiber: 3g; Sugar: 1g

Crab cakes

Ingredients:

- 1 egg
- 2 tbsp butter
- 1 tbsp cilantro, chopped
- 1/2 cup almond flour
- 4 tbsp pork rinds
- 1 lb. Crab meat
- 3 tsp ginger garlic paste
- 2 tsp sriracha
- 2 tsp lemon juice
- 1 tsp Dijon mustard
- 1/4 cup mayonnaise

Directions:

1. Add all ingredients except butter in a large bowl and mix until well combined.
2. Preheat the oven to 350 f.
3. Heat butter in a pan over medium-high heat.
4. Make crab cake from mixture and place in the pan and cook for 5 minutes.
5. Transfer pan in preheated oven and bake for 10 minutes.
6. Serve and enjoy.

Nutrition: Per Serves: Calories 251;Fat 16 g;Carbohydrates 7.4 g;Sugar 0.9 g;Protein 15 g;Cholesterol 97 mg

Herb pork chops

Servings: 4   **Cooking Time: 30 minutes**

Ingredients:

- 4 pork chops, boneless
- 1 tbsp olive oil
- 2 garlic cloves, minced
- 1 tsp dried rosemary, crushed
- 1 tsp oregano
- ½ tsp thyme
- 1 tbsp fresh rosemary, chopped
- ¼ tsp pepper
- ¼ tsp salt

Directions:

1. Preheat the oven 425 f.
2. Season pork chops with pepper and salt and set aside.
3. In a small bowl, mix together garlic, oil, rosemary, oregano, thyme, and fresh rosemary and rub over pork chops.
4. Place pork chops on baking tray and roast for 10 minutes.
5. Turn heat to 350 f and roast for 25 minutes more.
6. Serve and enjoy.

Nutrition: Per Serves: Calories 260;Fat 22 g;Carbohydrates 2.5 g;Sugar 0 g;Protein 19 g;Cholesterol 65 mg

Chili Garlic Salmon

Servings: 3   **Cooking Time: 2 minutes**

Ingredients:

- 1 lb salmon fillet, cut into three pieces
- 1 tsp red chili powder
- 1 garlic clove, minced
- 1 tsp ground cumin
- Pepper
- Salt

Directions:

1. Pour 1 1/2 cups water into the instant pot and place trivet into the pot.
2. In a small bowl, mix together chili powder, garlic, cumin, pepper, and salt.
3. Rub salmon pieces with spice mixture and place on top of the trivet.
4. Seal the instant pot with a lid and cook on steam mode for 2 minutes.
5. Once done, release pressure using the quick-release method than open the lid.
6. Serve and enjoy.

Nutrition: Per Serves: Calories 205 Fat 9 g Carbohydrates 1.1 g Sugar 0.1 g Protein 30 g Cholesterol 65 mg

Chicken Curry Wraps

Servings: 2   **Cooking Time: 10 minutes**

Ingredients:

- 1 cup cooked diced chicken
- 1/2 cup plain unsweetened yogurt
- 1 tablespoon skim milk, plus more if needed
- 1 celery stalk (diced)
- 1/2 teaspoon curry powder
- 1/4 teaspoon onion powder
- Salt and freshly ground black pepper, to taste
- 2 large green lettuce leaves
- 1 tablespoon slivered almonds (toasted)

Directions:

1. Mix chicken, yogurt, milk, celery, curry powder and onion powder and season to taste with salt and pepper.
2. Spread chicken mixture on lettuce leaves and sprinkle with almonds.
3. Roll up lettuce leaves burrito-style over chicken mixture. Serve immediately and enjoy!

Nutrition: Per Serves: Calories: 148; Total Fat: 5g; Saturated Fat: 1g; Protein: 23g; Carbs: 3g; Fiber: 1g; Sugar: 2g

Cauliflower Mash

🥣 **Servings: 4**   🍲 **Cooking Time: 10 minutes**

Ingredients:

- 1 lb. cauliflower, cut into florets
- 1/2 lemon juice
- 3 oz parmesan cheese, grated
- 4 oz butter
- Pepper
- Salt

Directions:

1. Boil cauliflower florets in the salted water until tender. Drain well.
2. Transfer cauliflower into the blender with remaining ingredients and blend until smooth.
3. Serve and enjoy.

Nutrition: Per Serves: Calories 300;Fat 27 g;Carbohydrates 7 g;Sugar 3 g;Protein 9 g;Cholesterol 75 mg

Buttery shrimp

🥣 **Servings: 4**   🍲 **Cooking Time: 15 minutes**

Ingredients:

- 1 1/2 lbs. Shrimp
- 1 tbsp Italian seasoning
- 1 lemon, sliced
- 1 stick butter, melted

Directions:

1. Add all ingredients into the large mixing bowl and toss well.
2. Transfer shrimp mixture on baking tray.
3. Bake at 350 f for 15 minutes.
4. Serve and enjoy.

Nutrition: Per Serves: Calories 415;Fat 26 g;Carbohydrates 3 g;Sugar 0.3 g;Protein 39 g;Cholesterol 421 mg

Broiled Fish Fillet

Servings: 2   **Cooking Time: 10 minutes**

Ingredients:

- 2 cod fish fillets
- 1/8 tsp curry powder
- 2 tsp butter
- 1/4 tsp paprika
- 1/8 tsp pepper
- 1/8 tsp salt

Directions:

1. Preheat the broiler.
2. Spray broiler pan with cooking spray and set aside.
3. In a small bowl, mix together paprika, curry powder, pepper, and salt.
4. Coat fish fillet with paprika mixture and place on broiler pan.
5. Broil fish for 10-12 minutes.
6. Top with butter and serve.

Nutrition: Per Serves: Calories 224 Fat 5.4 g Carbohydrates 0.3 g Sugar 0 g Protein 41.2 g Cholesterol 109 mg

Baked salmon

 Servings: 4   **Cooking Time: 35 minutes**

Ingredients:

- 1 lb. Salmon fillet
- 4 tbsp parsley, chopped
- 1/4 cup mayonnaise
- 1/4 cup parmesan cheese, grated
- 2 garlic cloves, minced
- 2 tbsp butter

Directions:

1. Preheat the oven to 350 f.
2. Place salmon on greased baking tray.
3. Melt butter in a pan over medium heat.
4. Add garlic and sauté for minute.
5. Add remaining ingredient and stir to combined.
6. Spread pan mixture over salmon fillet.
7. Bake for 20-25 minutes.
8. Serve and enjoy.

Nutrition: Per Serves: Calories 412;Fat 26 g;Carbohydrates 4.3 g;Sugar 1 g;Protein 34 g;Cholesterol 99 mg

Mediterranean Tuna Salad

🥣 **Servings: 4**   🍲 **Cooking Time: 30 minutes**

Ingredients:

- 1 small red onion (julienned)
- 1/4 cup vinegar
- 2 cans or jars (about 6 ounces each) Ventresca tuna (drained)
- 1 celery stalk (cut into thin 1" pieces)
- 1/4 cup pitted black olives (cut into strips)
- 1/4 cup chopped parsley leaves
- 1 tablespoon capers (halved if necessary)
- 1/4 cup extra-virgin olive oil
- 1 teaspoon lemon juice
- 1 teaspoon Worcestershire sauce
- 1 teaspoon fish sauce
- Salt and freshly ground black pepper, to taste

Directions:

1. Mix onion and vinegar and let stand for about 10 minutes.
2. In a large bowl, flake tuna into large chunks. Add celery, olives, parsley and capers and toss gently to combine.
3. Mix olive oil, lemon juice, Worcestershire sauce and fish sauce, drizzle over tuna mixture and toss gently to combine.
4. Drain onions and discard vinegar. Add onions to tuna mixture, season to taste with salt and pepper and toss gently to combine. Serve tuna salad immediately, or refrigerate until chilled through before serving. Enjoy!

Nutrition: Per Serves: Calories: 244; Total Fat: 18g; Saturated Fat: 2g; Protein: 14g; Carbs: 5g; Fiber: 2g; Sugar: 1g

Baked Lemon Tilapia

 Servings: 4   **Cooking Time: 12 minutes**

Ingredients:

- 4 tilapia fillets
- 2 tbsp fresh lemon juice
- 1 tsp garlic, minced
- 1/4 cup olive oil
- 2 tbsp fresh parsley, chopped
- 1 lemon zest
- Pepper
- Salt

Directions:

1. Preheat the oven to 425 F/ 220 C.
2. Spray a baking dish with cooking spray and set aside.
3. In a small bowl, whisk together olive oil, lemon zest, lemon juice, and garlic.
4. Season fish fillets with pepper and salt and place in the baking dish.
5. Pour olive oil mixture over fish fillets.
6. Bake fish fillets in the oven for 10-12 minutes.
7. Garnish with parsley and serve.

Nutrition: Per Serves: Calories 252 Fat 14.7 g Carbohydrates 0.5 g Sugar 0.2 g Protein 32.2 g Cholesterol 85 mg

Shrimp scampi

 Servings: 4   **Cooking Time: 10 minutes**

Ingredients:

- 1 lb. Shrimp
- 1/4 tsp red pepper flakes
- 1 tbsp fresh lemon juice
- 1/4 cup butter
- 1/2 cup chicken broth
- 2 garlic cloves, minced
- 1 shallot, sliced
- 3 tbsp olive oil
- 3 tbsp parsley, chopped
- Pepper
- Salt

Directions:

1. Heat oil in a pan over medium heat.
2. Add garlic and shallots and cook for 3 minutes.
3. Add broth, lemon juice, and butter and cook for 5 minutes.
4. Add red pepper flakes, parsley, pepper, and salt. Stir.
5. Add shrimp and cook for 3 minutes.
6. Serve and enjoy.

Nutrition: Per Serves: Calories 336;Fat 24 g;Carbohydrates 3 g;Sugar 0.2 g;Protein 26 g;Cholesterol 269 mg

Baked Cod Cups

Ingredients:

- 1 pound cod fillets
- 1 tablespoon butter (melted)
- 1 garlic clove (minced)
- 1 cup almond flour
- 4 eggs (beaten)
- 1/4 cup plain unsweetened yogurt
- 1 teaspoon chopped fresh dill
- 1 lemon (zested, juiced)
- 1 teaspoon baking powder
- Salt and freshly ground black pepper, to taste

Directions:

1. Preheat oven to 375°F. Line 12 wells of a muffin pan with foil liners and set aside.
2. Place cod fillets in a shallow microwave-safe dish. Brush about half of the butter over cod, sprinkle with garlic and cover dish. Micro-cook cod at high power for 3 minutes. Flip fillets, baste with butter and cook at high power until cod is flaky, 1 to 2 minutes more.
3. Flake cod with a fork and mix with the juices from the microwave dish, almond flour, eggs, yogurt, dill, lemon juice and baking powder. Season cod mixture to taste with salt and pepper and stir until thoroughly combined.
4. Spoon cod mixture into prepared muffin pan and bake until cod cups are cooked through and lightly golden brown, about 25 minutes. Garnish cod cups with lemon juice and serve immediately. Enjoy!

Nutrition: Per Serves: Calories: 110; Total Fat: 4g; Saturated Fat: 1g; Protein: 16g; Carbs: 2g; Fiber: 0g; Sugar: 0g

Spaghetti Squash Lasagna

 Servings: 6   **Cooking Time: 30 minutes**

Ingredients:

- 2 cup marinara sauce
- 3 cup roasted spaghetti squash
- 1 cup ricotta
- 8 tsps. grated parmesan cheese
- 6 oz. shredded mozzarella cheese
- ¼ tsp. red pepper flakes

Directions:

1. Set oven to preheat oven to 375 degrees F and spoon half of marinara sauce into baking dish.
2. Top with squash, then layer remaining Ingredients:.
3. Cover and set to bake until cheese is melted and edges brown (about 20 minutes).
4. Remove cover and return to bake for another 5 minutes. Enjoy!

Nutrition: Per Serves: Calories: 255, Fat: 15.9g , Carbs: 5.5g, Protein: 21.4g

Apple Cinnamon Oatmeal

 Servings: 1   **Cooking Time: 10 minutes**

Ingredients:

- 1/2 cup skim milk
- 1/3 cup water
- 1 apple (peeled, cored, diced)
- Dash of salt
- 1/2 cup old fashioned oats
- 1/4 teaspoon cinnamon
- 1/4 teaspoon vanilla

Directions:

1. Mix milk, water, apple and salt in a small saucepan and heat to a simmer, stirring occasionally (do not boil).
2. Add oats and cinnamon to saucepan and simmer, uncovered, for about 5 minutes, stirring occasionally.
3. Stir vanilla into oatmeal and serve immediately. Enjoy!

Nutrition: Per Serves: Calories: 184; Total Fat: 2g; Saturated Fat: 0g; Protein: 7g; Carbs: 36g; Fiber: 4g; Sugar: 19g

Sunshine Wrap

 Servings: 2   **Cooking Time: 30 minutes**

Ingredients:

- 8 oz. Grilled chicken breast
- ½ c. Diced celery
- 2/3 c. Mandarin oranges
- ¼ c. Minced onion
- 2 tbsps. Mayonnaise
- 1 tsp. Soy sauce
- ¼ tsp. Garlic powder
- ¼ tsp. Black pepper
- 1 whole wheat tortilla
- 4 lettuce leaves

Directions:

1. Combine all ingredients, except tortilla and lettuce, in a large bowl and toss to evenly coat.
2. Lay tortillas on a flat surface and cut into quarters.
3. Top each quarter with a lettuce leaf and spoon chicken mixture into the middle of each.
4. Roll each tortilla into a cone and seal by slightly wetting the edge with water. Enjoy!

Nutrition: Per Serves: Calories: 280.8, Fat: 21.1g, Carbs: 3g, Protein: 19g

Poultry Recipes

Grilled Chicken Wings

 Servings: 6   **Cooking Time: 20 minutes**

Ingredients:

- 1 and ½ pounds frozen chicken wings
- Fresh ground black pepper
- 1 teaspoon garlic powder
- 1 cup buffalo

Directions:

1. Pre-heat your grill to 350 degrees F.
2. Season wings with pepper and garlic powder, grill wings for 15 minutes per side.
3. Once they are browned and crispy, toss grilled wings in Buffalo wings sauce and olive oil.
4. Enjoy!

Nutrition: Per Serves: Calories: 180, Fat: 4g, Carbs: 36g, Protein: 4.5g

DZ's Grilled Chicken Wings

 Servings: 18   **Cooking Time: 20 minutes**

Ingredients:

- 1½ pounds frozen chicken wings
- Freshly ground black pepper
- 1 teaspoon garlic powder
- 1 cup buffalo wing sauce, such as Frank's RedHot
- 1 teaspoon extra-virgin olive oil
- Post-Op
- 2 or 3 wings

Directions:

1. Preheat the grill to 350°F.
2. Season the wings with the black pepper and garlic powder.
3. Grill the wings for 15 minutes per side. They will be browned and crispy when finished.
4. Toss the grilled wings in the buffalo wing sauce and olive oil.
5. Serve immediately.

Nutrition: Per Serves: Calories: 82; Total fat: 6g; Protein: 7g; Carbs: 1g; Fiber: 0g; Sugar: 0g; Sodium: 400mg

Chicken Thighs

Ingredients:

- 2 lbs. chicken thighs
- 2 medium onions, chopped
- 2 small chili peppers
- 1 cup chicken broth
- ¼ cup freshly squeezed orange juice, unsweetened
- 1 tsp orange extract, sugar-free
- 2 tbsp olive oil
- 1 tsp barbecue seasoning mix
- 1 small red onion, chopped

Directions:

1. Heat up the olive oil in a large saucepan. Add chopped onions and fry for several minutes, over a medium temperature – until golden color.
2. Combine chili peppers, orange juice and orange extract. Mix well in a food processor for 20-30 seconds. Add this mixture into a saucepan and stir well. Reduce heat to simmer.
3. Coat the chicken with barbecue seasoning mix and put into a saucepan. Add chicken broth and bring it to boil. Cook over a medium temperature until the water evaporates. Remove from the heat.
4. Preheat the oven to 350 degrees. Place the chicken into a large baking dish. Bake for about 15 minutes to get a nice crispy, golden brown color.

Nutrition: Per Serves: Net carbs 5.2 g;Fiber 0.9 g;Fats 16.2 g;Fatsr 3 g;Calories 357

Lemon Chicken

Ingredients:

- 2 teaspoons olive oil
- 2 boneless skinless chicken breasts
- 2 garlic cloves, minced
- 1 cup chicken stock
- 2 lemons, zested, juiced
- 1 teaspoon lemon pepper seasoning
- 1/2 teaspoon dried basil
- 1/2 teaspoon dried oregano
- Salt and freshly ground black pepper
- 1 tablespoon cornstarch
- 2 tablespoons cold water

Directions:

1. Heat olive oil in a large nonstick skillet over medium heat and sauté chicken just until cooked through, 7 to 8 minutes, stirring frequently.

2. Add garlic and sauté about 1 minute more, stirring constantly.Add chicken stock, lemon juice, lemon pepper, basil and oregano to chicken mixture and season to taste with salt and pepper. Reduce heat and simmer until chicken is cooked through and liquid is slightly reduced, 7 to 8 minutes, stirring occasionally.

3. Whisk cornstarch into cold water, add to skillet and stir gently until combined. Simmer until sauce is thickened, about 2 minutes, stirring constantly.

4. Transfer lemon chicken to a large bowl, sprinkle with lemon zest and serve immediately. Enjoy!

Nutrition: Per Serves: Net carbs 8 g;Fiber 1 g;Fats 5 g;Fatsr 2 g;Calories 134

Chicken Cordon Bleu

 Servings: 5   **Cooking Time: 30 minutes**

Ingredients:

- 6 chicken breasts, skinless, boneless, thinly sliced
- 6 slices lean deli ham
- 6 slices reduced-fat Swiss cheese, halved
- 2 large eggs
- 1 tablespoon water½ cup whole wheat bread crumbs
- 2 tablespoons Parmigiano-Reggiano cheese

Directions:

1. Pre-heat your oven to 450 degrees F.
2. Spray a baking sheet with cooking spray, pound chicken breasts to ¼ inch thickness.
3. Layer 1 slice ham and 1 slice (2 halves) cheese on each chicken breast.
4. Roll chicken and transfer them to the baking sheet (seam side down).
5. Take a small bowl and add whisk in eggs, take another bowl and mix in bread crumbs and cheese.
6. Use a pastry brush and lightly brush each chicken roll with egg wash. Sprinkle bread crumbs all over.
7. Bake for 30 minutes until the top is lightly browned.
8. Enjoy!

Nutrition: Per Serves: Net carbs 3 g;Fiber 1 g;Fats 7 g;Fatsr 4 g;Calories 174

Pulled Chicken

 Servings: 3   **Cooking Time: 8-10 hours**

Ingredients:

- 1 small onion, cut into strips
- 1 small bell pepper, strips
- 1 garlic clove, minced
- 1 tablespoon taco seasoning or barbecue spice rub
- 2 boneless skinless chicken breasts

Directions:

1. Arrange onion and bell pepper strips in the bottom of a 3- to 4-quart slow cooker and sprinkle with garlic.
2. Rub chicken breasts all over with taco seasoning and place in slow cooker.
3. Cover slow cooker and cook chicken on low until cooked through and tender, 8 to 10 hours.
4. Remove chicken from slow cooker and shred with two forks. Add juices from slow cooker to chicken and sprinkle with additional taco seasoning if desired. Serve immediately and enjoy!

Nutrition: Per Serves: Net carbs 7 g;Fiber 1 g;Fats 3 g;Fatsr 2 g;Calories 142

Chicken Caprese

Ingredients:

- 1 pound boneless skinless chicken breasts
- 2 tablespoons olive oil, divided
- 1 teaspoon garlic powder
- 1 teaspoon onion powder
- 1 teaspoon Italian herb seasoning
- Salt and freshly ground black pepper
- 1/2 cup grated mozzarella cheese
- 1 cup halved cherry tomatoes
- 2 tablespoons balsamic vinegar
- 2 tablespoons sliced fresh basil leaves

Directions:

1. Cut chicken breasts lengthwise into 1" thick slices and brush all over with about 1 tablespoon olive oil. Mix garlic powder, onion powder and herb seasoning, sprinkle over chicken and season to taste with salt and pepper.

2. Heat remaining 1 tablespoon olive oil in a large nonstick skillet over medium heat and cook chicken until lightly golden brown and no longer pink inside, 8 to 10 minutes, turning as necessary. Sprinkle mozzarella cheese over chicken and cook until cheese is melted, about 1 minute more.

3. Transfer chicken to a serving plate and arrange tomatoes over chicken. Drizzle balsamic vinegar over chicken, sprinkle with basil and serve immediately. Enjoy!

Nutrition: Per Serves: Net carbs 3 g;Fiber 1 g;Fats 9 g;Fatsr 4 g;Calories 170

Turkey Soup

Ingredients:

- 1 tablespoon butter
- 1 pound boneless skinless turkey thighs
- 6 cups chicken stock
- 1/2 teaspoon kosher salt, plus more to taste
- 1/4 teaspoon freshly ground black pepper
- 2 celery stalks, diced
- 2 carrots, peeled, diced
- 1 small onion, diced
- 1 1/2 teaspoons dried Italian herb seasoning
- 2 dried bay leaves

Directions:

1. Melt butter in a stock pot or large saucepan over medium heat and sauté turkey thighs until browned on all sides, about 5 minutes.

2. Add chicken stock, salt and pepper to pot and heat to a boil. Reduce heat, cover pot and simmer for about 10 minutes.

3. Add celery, carrots, onion, herb seasoning and bay leaves to pot, season to taste with salt and pepper and stir to combine. Cover pot and simmer until vegetables are tender, about 15 minutes more.

4. Remove bay leaves from soup and discard. Remove turkey thighs from soup, cut into bite-size pieces and stir back into soup. Serve soup immediately and enjoy!

Nutrition: Per Serves: Net carbs 4 g;Fiber 1 g;Fats 7 g;Fatsr 4 g;Calories 139

Buffalo Chicken Wrap

 Servings: 4   **Cooking Time: 10 minutes**

Ingredients:

- 3 cups rotisserie chicken breast
- 2 cups romaine lettuce, chopped
- 1 tomato, diced½ red onion, finely sliced
- ¼ cup buffalo wing sauce
- ¼ cup creamy peppercorn ranch dressing
- Chopped raw celery as for garnish
- 5 small whole grain low carb wraps

Directions:

1. Take a large mixing bowl and add chicken, lettuce, tomato, onion, wing sauce, dressing, and celery.
2. Add 1 cup of mixture onto each wrap and foil wrap over the salad.
3. Use a toothpick to secure the wrap, enjoy!

Nutrition: Per Serves: Net carbs 14 g;Fiber 3 g;Fats 7 g;Fatsr 1 g;Calories 200

Slow Cooker Turkey Chili

 Servings: 16   **Cooking Time: 8 hours**

Ingredients:

- Nonstick cooking spray
- 2 pounds extra-lean ground turkey
- 2 (14.5-ounce) cans kidney beans, drained and rinsed
- 1 (28-ounce) can diced tomatoes with green chiles
- 1 (8-ounce) can tomato puree
- 1 large onion, finely chopped
- 1 green bell pepper, finely chopped
- 2 celery stalks, finely chopped
- 4 teaspoons minced garlic
- 1 teaspoon dried oregano
- 2 tablespoons ground cumin
- 3 tablespoons chili powder
- 1 (8-ounce) can tomato juice
- Post-Op
- ¼ cup
- ¼ to ½ cup
- ½ to 1 cup

Directions:

1. Place a large skillet over medium-high heat and coat it with the cooking spray. Add the ground turkey. Using a wooden spoon, break it into smaller pieces and cook until browned, 7 to 9 minutes.
2. While the turkey browns, place the beans, tomatoes, tomato puree, onion, bell pepper, celery, garlic, oregano, cumin, chili powder, and tomato juice in the slow cooker. Stir in the cooked ground turkey and mix well.
3. Cover the slow cooker and turn on low to cook for 8 hours.
4. Serve garnished with Greek yogurt, shredded Cheddar cheese, and chopped scallions (if using).

Nutrition: Per Serves: Calories: 140; Total fat: 4g; Protein: 14g; Carbs: 12g; Fiber: 4g; Sugar: 4g; Sodium: 280mg

Fish and Seafood Recipes

Lemon Garlic Tilapia

 Servings: 4   🍲 **Cooking Time: 30 minutes**

Ingredients:

- 4 fillets, Tilapia
- 1 tablespoon, Olive oil
- 1 tablespoon, Margarine
- 1 tablespoon, Lemon juice
- ¼ teaspoon, Salt
- 1 teaspoon, Garlic salt
- 1 teaspoon, Parsley flakes, dried
- ¼ teaspoon, Cayenne pepperCooking spray

Directions:

1. Set the temperature of the oven at 400°F and start preheating.
2. Spray nonstick cooking oil onto the baking tray.
3. Put the butter into a nonstick saucepan and melt it on low-medium heat.
4. Now, add some lemon juice, salt, olive oil, garlic powder, and parsley into it and sauté for 3-4 minutes.
5. Place the tilapia fillets in the baking tray and pour the preparation on the top of the fillets.Now sprinkle some cayenne pepper on the fish.
6. Put in the oven and bake for about 12-13 minutes.
7. Flip sides and cook it for extra time.
8. Serve hot

Nutrition: Per Serves: Net carbs 1.8 g;Fiber 0.3 g;Fats 7.3 g;Fatsr 3 g;Calories 175.2

Herbed Salmon

🍲 **Servings: 2**   🍲 **Cooking Time: 15 minutes**

Ingredients:

- 2 salmon fillets
- 1/2 teaspoon onion powder
- 1/2 teaspoon garlic powder
- Salt and freshly ground black pepper
- 1 tablespoon olive oil1 can diced tomatoes
- 1 teaspoon Italian herb seasoning
- 2 tablespoons finely grated Parmesan cheese

Directions:

1. Preheat a medium nonstick skillet over medium heat. Brush salmon fillets with olive oil, sprinkle with onion and garlic powder and season to taste with salt and pepper. Sear fillets until browned on both sides, turning as necessary, 3 to 4 minutes

2. Pour undrained tomatoes over salmon fillets, sprinkle with herb seasoning and season to taste with salt and pepper. Heat to a boil, then reduce heat, cover and simmer until salmon is cooked through, 6 to 8 minutes.

3. Transfer salmon with sauce onto plates and sprinkle with Parmesan cheese to serve. Enjoy!

Nutrition: Per Serves: Net carbs 7 g;Fiber 2 g;Fats 10 g;Fatsr 1 g;Calories 227

Herb-Crusted Salmon Fillets

 Servings: 4   **Cooking Time: 10 minutes**

Ingredients:

- 16 ounces, Atlantic salmon
- 2 tablespoons, Chives, roughly chopped
- 2 tablespoons, Parsley, chopped
- 1 cup, Breadcrumbs, whole-grain
- ½ teaspoon, Garlic powder
- ½ teaspoon, Onion powder
- 1 teaspoon, Lemon peel, grated
- ¼ cup, Lemon juice¼ teaspoon, Salt
- ½ teaspoon, Pepper
- Cooking spray.

Directions:

1. Preheat the oven on high heat at 400°F.
2. Line the baking tray with a baking paper and spray some cooking oil.
3. Season the salmon fillets with pepper and salt.
4. Place the salmon on the baking tray, skin side down facing the baking liner.Put all the ingredients except lemon juice in mixer bowl.
5. Combine well until it becomes a smooth mix.
6. Drizzle some lemon juice on the salmon fillets and spread the breadcrumb mixture over the salmon fillets.
7. Spray evenly with cooking spray, and bake it at least for 10 - 15 minutes.
8. Serve hot.

Nutrition: Per Serves: Net carbs 7.2 g;Fiber 1.1 g;Fats 14.4 g;Fatsr 2 g;Calories 259.5

Lime Shrimp

 Servings: 2   **Cooking Time: 10 minutes**

Ingredients:

- 28 Shrimps, ready to cook
- 1 tablespoon, Lime juice
- 1/8 teaspoon, Salt
- ¾ teaspoon, Black pepper
- 2 tablespoons, Chopped onion
- Cooking spray

Directions:

1. Spray some cooking oil into the skillet.
2. Bring the skillet to medium heat.
3. When the skillet becomes hot, put all the ingredients and sauté occasionally until the onions and shrimps get cooked well.
4. Serve hot

Nutrition: Per Serves: Net carbs 2.2 g;Fiber 0.4 g;Fats 0.9 gSugar 1 g;Calories 84.4

Grilled Lemon Shrimps

 Servings: 3   **Cooking Time: 6 minutes**

Ingredients:

- 1 lb. fresh shrimps, cleaned
- 1 tbsp fresh rosemary
- 4 tbsp extra-virgin olive oil
- 1 tsp garlic powder
- 2 tbsp lemon juice, freshly squeezed
- ½ tsp salt
- ½ tsp black pepper, freshly ground
- ½ tsp dried thyme, ground
- ½ tsp dried oregano, ground
- 1 organic lemon, sliced into wedges

Directions:

1. Combine olive oil, garlic, lemon juice, salt, pepper, thyme, and oregano in a medium bowl and mix until well incorporated. Place the shrimp and coat evenly with the marinade mixture. Cover the bowl and chill for at least 1 hour to marinate the shrimps.
2. Preheat the grill to a medium-high temperature. Brush the grill grids with some oil.
3. Insert 2 to 3 shrimps on each skewer, brush with marinade and grill for 3 minutes. Turn and grill the other side for another 3 minutes. Transfer to a serving platter.
4. Serve warm with lemons wedges and sprinkle with chopped parsley.

Nutrition: Per Serves: Net carbs 6.2 g;Fiber 2 g;Fats 21.6 g;Fatsr 3 g;Calories 357

Microwave Grilled Salmon

Ingredients:

- 1½ pound, Salmon
- 2 tablespoons, Olive oil
- 1 tablespoon, Lemon juice1
  clove, Garlic, minced
- ¼ teaspoon, Salt¼ teaspoon,
  Ground pepper

Directions:

1. Set your microwave to grill cooking.
2. In a medium bowl, mix all the ingredients.
3. Marinate the salmon.
4. Grill the fish.
5. Serve hot.

Nutrition: Per Serves: Net carbs 0.4 g;Fiber 1 g;Fats 9.5 g;Fatsr 2 g;Calories 210.2

Easy Baked Salmon

 Servings: 4   **Cooking Time: 15 minutes**

Ingredients:

- 4 salmon fillets
- 1 lemon zest
- 1 tsp sea salt
- 3 oz olive oil
- 1 garlic clove, minced
- 1 tsp fresh dill, chopped
- 1 tbsp fresh parsley, chopped
- 1/8 tsp white pepper

Directions:

1. Preheat the oven at 200 C.
2. Place all ingredients except salmon fillet in microwave safe bowl and microwave for 45 seconds.
3. Stir well until combine.
4. Place salmon fillets on parchment lined baking dish.
5. Spread evenly olive oil and herb mixture over the each salmon fillet.
6. Place in preheated oven and bake for 15 minutes.
7. Serve and enjoy.

Nutrition: Per Serves: Net carbs 0.5 g;Fiber 3.1 gFats 30.9 gSugar 1 g;Calories 408

Slowly Roasted Pesto Salmon

Servings: 4   **Cooking Time: 20 minutes**

Ingredients:

- 4 salmon fillets
- 1 teaspoon extra-virgin olive oil
- 4 tablespoons basil pesto

Directions:

1. Pre-heat your oven to 275 degrees F.
2. Line a rimmed baking sheet with foil and brush with olive oil.
3. Transfer salmon fillets skin-side down on a baking sheet and spread 1 tablespoon pesto on each fillet.
4. Roast for 20 minutes.
5. Serve and enjoy!

Nutrition: Per Serves: Calories: 180, Fat: 4g, Carbs: 36g, Protein: 4.5g

Broiled White Fish Parmesan

Servings: 4   **Cooking Time: 10 minutes**

Ingredients:

- 3 ounces, Codfish
- ¼ cup, Parmesan cheese, grated
- 2 tablespoons, Light margarine, softened
- 1/8 teaspoon, Garlic salt
- 1/8 teaspoon, Ground black pepper
- 1 tablespoon, Lemon juice
- 1 tablespoon and 1½ teaspoons, Mayonnaise
- 1/8 teaspoon, Dried basil
- 1/8teaspoon, Onion powder
- Cooking spray

Directions:

1. Set the grill on high temperature and preheat before start cooking.
2. Grease the broiling pot with cooking spray.
3. Combine butter, Parmesan cheese, lemon juice and mayonnaise.
4. Season it with pepper, onion powder, dried basil, and garlic salt.
5. Mix it well and keep ready to use.
6. Layer the fillets on the broiler pan and broil for 2-3 minutes.
7. Flip it and cook for another 2-3 minutes.
8. Remove the baked fillets from the grill onto a plate and transfer the Parmesan mixture over it.
9. Again, broil it for a couple of minutes until the topping becomes brown.
10. Serve hot, when the flakes can easily remove.

Nutrition: Per Serves: Net carbs 1 g;Fiber 1 g;Fats 8.2 g;Fatsr 2 g;Calories 197.1 g

Tuna Salad

Servings: 4   **Cooking Time: 10 minutes**

Ingredients:

- 2 pounds, Tuna cooked
- 1 stalk, Celery, finely chopped
- 2/3 cup, Cottage cheese, non-fat
- 4 tablespoons, Plain yogurt, low-fat
- ¼, Small onion, red, coarsely chopped
- 1 teaspoon, Dijon mustard1 teaspoon, Lemon juice
- ¼ teaspoon, Dill
- ½ teaspoon, Salt

Directions:

1. In a large bowl, mix all the ingredients to make the salad.
2. Ideal for making sandwiches.

Nutrition: Per Serves: Net carbs 11.7 gFiber 0.6 g;Fats 2.2 g;Fatsr 1 g;Calories 190.3

Vegan Recipes

Grilled Cheese Pizza Sandwich

 Servings: 1   **Cooking Time: 5 minutes**

Ingredients:

- 2 slices, multi-grain bread
- 2 tablespoons, marinara sauce
- 1 teaspoon, shredded parmesan
- ¼ cup, mozzarella cheese
- ¼ teaspoon, pepper ground
- ¼ teaspoon, salt

Directions:

1. Spread the marinara sauce on one side of both bread slice.
2. Now spread mozzarella cheese on top of one slice bread.
3. Sprinkle grated parmesan cheese on the top of the mozzarella.
4. Top it with 2nd piece of bread, keeping the sauce side down.
5. Now place it on a heated pan until the cheese starts to melt and the outer side becomes golden brown.
6. Serve hot.

Nutrition: Per Serves: Net carbs 26.3 g Fiber 4.4 g Fats 8.3 g Sugar 6 g Calories 242.3

Mashed Cauliflower

Ingredients:

- 1 large head cauliflower, cored
- 1/2 cup skim milk
- 1/4 teaspoon garlic powder
- 1/4 teaspoon onion powder
- Salt and freshly ground black pepper

Directions:

1. Pour water into a large saucepan to a depth of about 2 inches. Set steamer basket in saucepan and place cauliflower in basket. Cover pan and steam over medium heat until cauliflower is soft, 10 to 12 minutes.

2. Carefully remove cauliflower from steamer basket and place in a large bowl. Crumble and lightly mash cauliflower with a fork.

3. Add milk, garlic powder and onion powder to cauliflower and puree with an immersion blender until smooth or to desired consistency, adding more milk if needed.

4. Season cauliflower to taste with salt and pepper and serve . Enjoy!

Nutrition: Per Serves: Calories: 180, Fat: 4g, Carbs: 36g, Protein: 4.5g

Fresh Tomato and Celery Soup

🥣 **Servings: 4**   🍲 **Cooking Time: 30 minutes**

Ingredients:

- 1 lb. tomatoes, peeled, roughly chopped
- 4 oz celery root, finely chopped
- ¼ cup fresh celery leaves, finely chopped
- 1 tbsp fresh basil, finely chopped
- Salt and pepper
- 5 tbsp extra virgin olive oil

Directions:

1. Preheat the oil in a large non-stick frying pan over a medium-high temperature.
2. Add finely chopped celery root, celery leaves, and fresh basil. Season with salt and pepper and stir-fry for about 10 minutes, until nicely browned.Add chopped tomatoes and about ¼ cup of water. Reduce the heat to minimum and cook for 15 minutes, stirring constantly, until softened. Now add about 4 cups of water (or vegetable broth) and bring it to a boil. Give it a good stir and remove from the heat.
3. Top with fresh parsley and serve.

Nutrition: Per Serves: Net carbs 6.9 g;Fiber 1.9 g;Fats 10.8 g;Fatsr 2 g;Calories 122

Mini Eggplant Pizzas

 Servings: 4   **Cooking Time: 12 minutes**

Ingredients:

- 1 eggplant
- ¼ cup, pasta sauce
- 4 teaspoons, olive oil
- ½ teaspoon, salt
- 1/8 teaspoon, ground black pepper
- ½ cup, shredded part-skim mozzarella cheese
- Cooking spray
- Baking sheet

Directions:

1. Peel eggplant and cut into 4 half-inch-thick slices.
2. Preheat your toaster at 425°f.
3. Brush both parts of the eggplant with some cooking spray oil and season it with pepper and salt.
4. Arrange the pizza on a baking sheet and bake for 8 minutes, until it becomes browned and tender.
5. Flip sides and bake further 6 - 8 minutes.
6. Spread 1 tbsp of pasta sauce on all side of the sliced eggplant.
7. Top it with the shredded cheese.
8. Bake the cheese until it starts to melt for about 3 - 5 minutes.
9. Serve the dish hot.

Nutrition: Per Serves: Net carbs 8.9 g Fiber 3.2 g Fats 7.5 g Sugar 8 g Calories 119.1

Cheesy Cauliflower Casserole

 Servings: 8   **Cooking Time: 45 minutes**

Ingredients:

- 1 head cauliflower, cut into florets
- 1 cup low-fat cottage cheese
- 1 cup low-fat plain Greek yogurt
- ½ teaspoon Dijon mustard
- ¼ teaspoon garlic powder
- 2 ounces (½ cup) shredded aged white Cheddar cheese
- 2 ounces (½ cup) shredded mild Cheddar cheese
- Post-Op
- ½ cup
- ½ to 1 cup serving

Directions:

1. Preheat the oven to 350°F.
2. Fill a medium pot one-third full with water, and place a steamer basket inside. Bring the water to a boil over high heat.
3. Add the cauliflower to the steamer basket, cover the pot, and reduce the heat to a gentle boil. Steam the cauliflower for 10 to 15 minutes, or until the florets are soft. Alternatively, you can steam the cauliflower with 2 tablespoons of water in the microwave on high for about 4 minutes, or until tender.
4. While the cauliflower steams, mix together the cottage cheese, yogurt, mustard, and garlic powder in a medium bowl.
5. Drain the cauliflower in a large colander, and gently mash it with a potato masher to drain out excess water.
6. Stir the cauliflower pieces into the cottage cheese mixture. Add the Cheddar cheeses and mix well.
7. Transfer the cauliflower mixture to an 8-by-8-inch or 11-by-7-inch baking dish. Bake for about 30 minutes. It is done when the edges begin to brown.
8. Serve immediately.

Nutrition: Per Serves: Calories: 147; Total fat: 7g; Protein: 13g; Carbs: 8g; Fiber: 2g; Sugar: 4g; Sodium: 263g

Mini Vegetable Frittatas

 Servings: 9   **Cooking Time: 15 minutes**

Ingredients:

- 5 Eggs
- 2 ounces Goat cheese, shredded
- 2 tablespoons Low-fat milk
- 1 cup Tomato, chopped
- 2 cups Chopped broccoli, fresh
- Ingredients from the kitchen store:
- ¼ teaspoon Pepper crushed
- ¼ teaspoon Salt
- Cooking spray

Directions:

1. Blend milk and eggs in a mixer bowl.
2. Add crumbled goat cheese and all the chopped vegetables in it and combine.
3. Season it with pepper and salt.
4. Spoon this mixture into muffin cups sprayed with cooking oil.
5. Bake it at 350°F for about 12-15 minutes until it becomes golden color on the top.
6. Serve hot.

Nutrition: Per Serves: Net carbs 3.9 g;Fiber 1.4 g;Fats 4.03 g;Fatsr 1 g;Calories 71.3

Blue Oatmeal Porridge

 Servings: 2   **Cooking Time: 5 minutes**

Ingredients:

- 1 cup, whole grain oatmeal
- 2 tablespoons, flaxseed meal, ground flax
- ½ tablespoon, dry cocoa powder, unsweetened
- 2 teaspoon, brown sugar
- ½ cup, blueberries, frozen, unsweetened
- 1½ cup, water

Directions:

1. Boil water in a pan.
2. Combine all of the dry ingredients in a mixing bowl and add to the boiling water.
3. Reduce the temperature and cook it for a couple of minutes as far as you get the desired consistency.
4. Top it with blueberries at the time of serving.

Nutrition: Per Serves: Net carbs 38.4 g Fiber 7 g Fats 5.7 g Sugar 1 g Calories 214.2

Red Lentil Soup with Kale

 Servings: 6   **Cooking Time: 45 minutes**

Ingredients:

- 1 tablespoon extra-virgin olive oil
- 1 cup chopped onion
- ½ cup carrots, cut into ½-inch chunks
- ½ cup celery, cut into ¼-inch chunks
- 1 teaspoon minced garlic
- 1 cup red lentils
- 1 teaspoon dried thyme
- 1 teaspoon ground cumin
- 2 cups low-sodium vegetable broth
- 2 cups water
- 2 large stalks kale, stemmed, with leaves chopped (about 2 cups)
- 1 bay leaf
- 2 tablespoons freshly squeezed lemon juice
- Low-fat plain Greek yogurt (optional)
- Post-Op
- ¼ cup
- ½ cup
- 1 to 2 cups

Directions:

1. In a large stock pot over medium heat, heat the olive oil. Add the onion, carrots, celery, and garlic, and sauté until tender, 5 to 7 minutes.
2. Add the lentils, thyme, and cumin. Mix well and stir for 1 to 2 minutes, until all the ingredients are coated well with the seasonings.
3. Add the broth and water to the pot. Bring to a simmer, add the kale, and stir well. Add the bay leaf, then cover the pot and simmer for 30 to 35 minutes.
4. Remove the pot from the heat. Remove and discard the bay leaf. Stir in the lemon juice. Use an immersion blender to puree the soup to your desired consistency. Alternatively, let the soup cool for 10 minutes before pureeing it in batches in a blender.
5. Garnish each bowl of soup with a dollop of the Greek yogurt (if using) and serve.

Nutrition: Per Serves: Calories: 170; Total fat: 3g; Protein: 13g; Carbs: 24g; Fiber: 3g; Sugar: 4g; Sodium: 59mg

Barley-Mushroom Risotto

 Servings: 6   **Cooking Time: 55 minutes**

Ingredients:

- 1 tablespoon extra-virgin olive oil
- 1 teaspoon minced garlic
- 2 leeks, cleaned, ends removed and finely chopped, both white and green parts
- 4 cups sliced mushrooms
- 2 teaspoons dried thyme
- ½ cup pearl barley
- ½ cup dry white wine
- 1½ cups low-sodium vegetable or chicken broth
- 1 cup water
- 3 cups fresh spinach leaves
- Post-Op
- ½ cup

Directions:

1. Place a large skillet over medium heat. Sauté the olive oil and garlic for 1 minute. Add the leeks and sauté for 2 to 3 minutes, or until tender.
2. Add the mushrooms and cook until tender and browned, about 4 minutes.
3. Stir in the thyme and barley. Cook for another 2 minutes.
4. Add the wine and stir. Simmer for about 5 minutes, or until the liquid is absorbed.
5. Add the broth and water. Reduce the heat to low, cover the skillet, and simmer for 40 minutes. Stir occasionally to make sure the barley does not stick to the bottom of the pan.
6. Gently stir in the spinach and mix until it is wilted. Serve immediately.

Nutrition: Per Serves: Calories: 104; Total fat: 3g; Protein: 3g; Carbs: 16g; Fiber: 3g; Sugar: 1g; Sodium: 40mg

Saucy Garlic Broccoli

Ingredients:

- 2 stalks broccoli
- Salt and freshly ground black pepper
- 1 tablespoon olive oil
- 2 garlic cloves, minced
- 1 tablespoon ginger, minced
- 2 cups chicken stock
- 2 tablespoons soy sauce
- 1/2 teaspoon red pepper flakes
- 2 tablespoons cornstarch
- 1/4 cup chopped salted cashews

Directions:

1. Pour water into a large saucepan to a depth of about 2 inches. Set steamer basket in saucepan, place broccoli in basket and season to taste with salt and pepper. Cover pan and steam over medium heat until broccoli is soft, 8 to 10 minutes.

2. Transfer broccoli to a serving dish, cover to keep warm and set aside. Empty cooking water from pan.

3. For the sauce, in the same pan, heat oil over medium heat and sauté garlic and ginger for about 1 minute. Add chicken broth, soy sauce and red pepper flakes to pan, season to taste with salt and pepper and heat to a simmer, stirring occasionally, about 10 minutes.

4. Dissolve cornstarch in about 1/4 cup cold water, whisk into sauce and cook until sauce is thickened, stirring constantly, about 2 minutes.

5. Pour sauce over broccoli and stir gently to coat. Sprinkle cashews over broccoli and serve immediately. Enjoy!

Nutrition: Per Serves: Net carbs 32 g;Fiber 3 g;Fats 12 g;Fatsr 1 g;Calories 232

Sides, Snacks & Desserts Recipes

Chia almond pudding

🍲 **Servings: 4**   🍲 **Cooking Time: 5 minutes**

Ingredients:

- 2 tbsp almonds, toasted and crushed
- 1/3 cup chia seeds
- ½ tsp vanilla
- 4 tbsp erythritol
- ¼ cup unsweetened cocoa powder
- 2 cups unsweetened almond milk

Directions:

1. Add almond milk, vanilla, sweetener, and cocoa powder into the blender and blend until well combined.
2. Pour blended mixture into the bowl.
3. Add chia seeds and whisk for 1-2 minutes.
4. Pour pudding mixture into the serving bowls and place in fridge for 1-2 hours.
5. Top with crushed almonds and serve.

Nutrition: Per Serves: Calories 170;Fat 12 g;Carbohydrates 12 g;Sugar 1 g;Protein 7 g;Cholesterol 35 mg

Green Tea Smoothie

 Servings: 2   **Cooking Time: 10 minutes**

Ingredients:

- 3 tbsp green tea powder
- 1 cup grapes, white
- ½ cup kale, finely chopped
- 1 tbsp honey
- ½ tsp fresh mint, ground
- 1 cup water

Directions:

1. Rinse the grapes under cold running water. Drain and remove the pits. Set aside.
2. Place kale in a large colander and wash thoroughly under cold running water. Drain well and finely chop it into small pieces. Set aside.
3. Combine green tea powder with 2 tablespoons of hot water. Soak for 2 minutes. Set aside.
4. Now, combine grapes, kale, honey, mint, and water in a blender and process until well combined. Stir in the water and tea mixture.
5. Refrigerate 30 minutes before serving.
6. Enjoy!

Nutrition: Per Serves: Net carbs 18.3 g Fiber 2.2 g Fats 0.2 g Sugar 1 g Calories 76

Frozen Berry Yogurt

 Servings: 6   **Cooking Time: 5 minutes**

Ingredients:

- 4 cups frozen blackberries
- 1 tsp vanilla
- 1 tbsp fresh lemon juice
- 1 cup full-fat yogurt

Directions:

1. Add all ingredients into the blender and blend until smooth.
2. Pour blended mixture into the container. Cover and place in the refrigerator for 2 hours.
3. Serve and enjoy.

Nutrition: Per Serves: Calories 60 Fat 0.9 g Carbohydrates 11.6 g Sugar 7 g Protein 1.8 g Cholesterol 0 mg

Chocó Protein Balls

 Servings: 15   **Cooking Time: 10 minutes**

Ingredients:

- 1 tbsp unsweetened cocoa powder
- 1 tsp vanilla
- 3 tbsp pistachios, chopped
- 1/3 cup chia seeds
- 1 cup almond butter
- 1 ½ cup oats

Directions:

1. Line baking tray with parchment paper and set aside.
2. Add all ingredients into the mixing bowl and mix until well combined.
3. Make small balls from mixture and place on a prepared tray and place it in the refrigerator for overnight.
4. Serve and enjoy.

Nutrition: Per Serves: Calories 55 Fat 2.4 g Carbohydrates 6.7 g Sugar 0.2 g Protein 2.1 g Cholesterol 0 mg

Chia Seed Pudding

 Servings: 4   **Cooking Time: 5 minutes**

Ingredients:

- ½ cup chia seeds
- 1 tsp liquid stevia
- 1 ½ tsp pumpkin pie spice
- ½ cup pumpkin puree
- ¾ cup unsweetened coconut milk
- ¾ cup full-fat coconut milk

Directions:

1. Add all ingredients into the mixing bowl and whisk well to combine.
2. Pour into the serving bowls and place them in the refrigerator for 2 hours.
3. Serve and enjoy.

Nutrition: Per Serves: Calories 275 Fat 24.5 g Carbohydrates 9.9 g Sugar 3.3 g Protein 5.3 g Cholesterol 0 mg

Cheesy radish

Ingredients:

- 16 oz. Monterey jack cheese, shredded
- 2 cups radish
- ½ cup heavy cream
- 1 teaspoon lemon juice
- Salt and white pepper, to taste

Directions:

1. Preheat the oven to 3000f and lightly grease a baking sheet.
2. Heat heavy cream in a small saucepan and season with salt and white pepper.
3. Stir in monterey jack cheese and lemon juice.
4. Place the radish on the baking sheet and top with the cheese mixture.
5. Bake for about 45 minutes and remove from the oven to serve hot.

Nutrition: Per Serves: Calories 387;Total fat 32g;Saturated fat 20.1g 1;Cholesterol 97mg;Sodium 509mg;Total carbohydrate 2.6g;Dietary fiber 0.7g;Total sugars 1.3g;Protein 22.8g

Cheesecake fat bombs

 Servings: 24 **Cooking Time: 10 minutes**

Ingredients:

- 8 oz cream cheese
- 1 ½ tsp vanilla
- 2 tbsp erythritol
- 4 oz coconut oil
- 4 oz heavy cream

Directions:

1. Add all ingredients into the mixing bowl and beat using immersion blender until creamy.
2. Pour batter into the mini cupcake liner and place in refrigerator until set.
3. Serve and enjoy.

Nutrition: Per Serves: Calories 90;Fat 9.8 g;Carbohydrates 1.4 g;Sugar 0.1 g;Protein 0.8 g;Cholesterol 17 mg

Caprese snack

Servings: 4 **Cooking Time: 5 minutes**

Ingredients:

- 8 oz. Mozzarella, mini cheese balls
- 8 oz. Cherry tomatoes
- 2 tablespoons green pesto
- Salt and black pepper, to taste
- 1 tablespoon garlic powder

Directions:

1. Slice the mozzarella balls and tomatoes in half.
2. Stir in the green pesto and season with garlic powder, salt and pepper to serve.

Nutrition: Per Serves: Calories 407;Total fat 34.5g;Saturated fat 7.4g;Cholesterol 30mg;Sodium 343mg;Total carbohydrate 6.3g;Dietary fiber 0.9g;Total sugars 2g;Protein 19.4g

Jicama fries

Ingredients:

- 2 tablespoons avocado oil
- 1 jicama, cut into fries
- 1 tablespoon garlic powder
- ½ cup parmesan cheese, grated
- Salt and black pepper, to taste

Directions:

1. Preheat the air fryer to 4000f and grease the fryer basket.
2. Boil jicama fries for about 10 minutes and drain well.
3. Mix jicama fries with garlic powder, salt and black pepper in a bowl.
4. Place in the fryer basket and cook for about 10 minutes.
5. Dish onto a platter and serve warm.

Nutrition: Per Serves: Calories 145;Total fat 7.8g;Saturated fat 4.4g;Cholesterol 20mg;Sodium 262mg;Total carbohydrate 10.4g;Dietary fiber 4g;Total sugars 2.6g;Protein 10.4g

Beet Spinach Salad

 Servings: 3 **Cooking Time: 40 minutes**

Ingredients:

- 2 medium-sized beet, trimmed, sliced
- 1 cup fresh spinach, chopped
- 2 spring onions, finely chopped
- 1 small green apple, cored, chopped
- 3 tbsp olive oil
- 2 tbsp fresh lime juice
- 1 tbsp honey, raw
- 1 tsp apple cider vinegar
- 1 tsp salt

Directions:

1. Wash the beets and trim off the green parts. Set aside.
2. Wash the spinach thoroughly and drain. Cut into small pieces and set aside.
3. Wash the apple and cut lengthwise in half. Remove the core and cut into bite-sized pieces and set aside.
4. Wash the onions and cut into small pieces. Set aside.
5. In a small bowl, combine olive oil, lime juice, honey, vinegar, and salt. Stir until well incorporated and set aside to allow flavors to meld.
6. Place the beets in a deep pot. Pour enough water to cover and cook for about 40 minutes, or until tender. Remove the skin and slice. Set aside.
7. In a large salad bowl, combine beets, spinach, spring onions, and apple. Stir well until combined and drizzle with previously prepared dressing. Give it a good final stir and serve immediately.

Nutrition: Per Serves: Net carbs 23.8 g;Fiber 3.6 g;Fats 14.3 g;Fatsr 5 g;Calories 215

Low carb onion rings

 Servings: 6   **Cooking Time: 30 minutes**

Ingredients:

- 2 medium white onions, sliced into ½ inch thick rings
- ½ cup coconut flour
- 4 large eggs
- 4 oz pork rinds
- 1 cup parmesan cheese, grated

Directions:

1. Preheat an air fryer to 3900f and grease a fryer basket.
2. Put coconut flour in one bowl, eggs in the second bowl and pork rinds and parmesan cheese in the third bowl.
3. Coat the onion rings through the three bowls one by one and repeat.
4. Place the coated onion rings in the fryer basket and cook for about 15 minutes.
5. Dish out to a platter and serve with your favorite low carb sauce.

Nutrition: Per Serves: Calories 270;Total fat 15.1g;Saturated fat 7.1g;Cholesterol 164mg;Sodium 586mg;Total carbohydrate 11g;Dietary fiber 4.8g;Total sugars 1.8g;Protein 24.1g

Basil parmesan tomatoes

 Servings: 6   **Cooking Time: 30 minutes**

Ingredients:

- ½ teaspoon dried oregano
- 4 roma tomatoes
- Spices: onion powder, garlic powder, sea salt and black pepper
- ½ cup parmesan cheese, shredded
- 12 small fresh basil leaves

Directions:

1. Preheat the oven to 4250f and grease a baking sheet lightly.
2. Mix together dried oregano, onion powder, garlic powder, sea salt and black pepper in a small bowl.
3. Arrange the tomato slices on a baking sheet and sprinkle with the seasoning blend.
4. Top with parmesan cheese and basil leaves and transfer to the oven.
5. Bake for about 20 minutes and remove from the oven to serve.

Nutrition: Per Serves: Calories 49;Total fat 2.2g;Saturated fat 1.4g;Cholesterol 7mg;Sodium 91mg;Total carbohydrate 4.3g;Dietary fiber 1.2g;Total sugars 2.4g;Protein 3.9g

Mix berry sorbet

 Servings: 1   **Cooking Time: 10 minutes**

Ingredients:

- ½ cup raspberries, frozen
- ½ cup blackberries, frozen
- 1 tsp liquid stevia
- 6 tbsp water

Directions:

1. Add all ingredients into the blender and blend until smooth.
2. Pour blended mixture into the container and place in refrigerator until harden.
3. Servings chilled and enjoy.

Nutrition: Per Serves: Calories 63;Fat 0.8 g;Carbohydrates 14 g;Sugar 6 g;Protein 1.7 g;Cholesterol 0 mg

Avocado Hummus

 Servings: 4   **Cooking Time: 5 minutes**

Ingredients:

- ½ avocado, chopped
- 2 tbsp olive oil
- ½ tsp onion powder
- 1 tsp tahini
- ½ tsp garlic, minced
- 1 tbsp lemon juice
- 1 cup frozen edamame, thawed
- Pepper
- Salt

Directions:

1. Add all ingredients into the blender and blend until smooth.
2. Serve with vegetables.

Nutrition: Per Serves: Calories 215 Fat 17 g Carbohydrates 10 g Sugar 0.3 g Protein 9.1 g Cholesterol 0 mg

Red Orange Salad

Servings: 3   **Cooking Time: 20 minutes**

Ingredients:

- Fresh lettuce leaves, rinsed
- 1 small cucumber sliced
- ½ red bell pepper, sliced
- 1 cup frozen seafood mix
- 1 onion, peeled, finely chopped
- 3 garlic cloves, crushed
- ¼ cup fresh orange juice
- 5 tbsp extra virgin olive oil
- Salt to taste

Directions:

1. Heat up 3 tbsp of extra virgin olive oil over medium-high temperature. Add chopped onion and crushed garlic. Stir fry for about 5 minutes.

2. Reduce the heat to minimum and add 1 cup of frozen seafood mix. Cover and cook for about 15 minutes, until soft. Remove from the heat and allow it to cool for a while.

3. Meanwhile, combine the vegetables in a bowl. Add the remaining 2 tbsp of olive oil, fresh orange juice and a little salt. Toss well to combine.

4. Top with seafood mix and serve immediately.

Nutrition: Per Serves: Net carbs 13.1 g;Fiber 1.8 g;Fats 14.6 g;Fatsr 4 g;Calories 206

Printed in Great Britain
by Amazon

31676944R00051